Gofors & Grumps

Book four

T-Z

An A-Z of Bible Characters by **Derek Prime**

with illustrations by **Ruth Goodridge**

DayOnepublicati

Copyright © Derek Prime 1995
First printed 1995

ISBN 0 902548 60 3

Published by Day One Publications
6 Sherman Road, Bromley, Kent BR1 3JH

Designed by Steve Devane and printed by Clifford Frost Ltd, Wimbledon SW19 2SE

Gofors & Grumps

T-Z

DayOnepublications

Mr **Thoughtful**

I wonder if you are a thoughtful or a thought-less person? A thoughtful person is 'full of thought', someone who thinks of how he can or she can help or serve others.

A thoughtless person on the other hand is some-one who does not think very much about other people and their feelings.

A school teacher told her class to notice how many bad spellings they could find on their way home from school. Opposite the school there was a shop with prices of things written on its win-dows.

As soon as the girls looked they saw many mis-takes. They sat down and started writing them all down. They giggled. 'Oh, there's another one,' and they laughed triumphantly, 'only one l, in woollens.' 'Look, how he's spelt cardigan with a 'k'!' 'And trousers with two o's.' They thought it was great fun.

Then the old man who owned the shop came out, looked at them and at the shop window and asked what they were doing. 'We're writing down all your spelling mistakes - the teacher told us.'

There was silence. He did not chase them away. Instead his face turned crimson, and he went back into his shop without a word. The girls suddenly felt sick - they had been thoughtless. It is never

Something to do

Mark the map!
Find where Ephesus
and Rome are on the
map on page 47 and
write in their names.

kind to make fun of other people's mistakes.

I wonder if you and I are ever thoughtless? Let me tell you about Mr. Thoughtful, whose real name was Onesiphorus.

He lived at one time in Ephesus, the most important city in the Roman province of Asia, on the west coast of what is now Asiatic Turkey.

The apostle Paul stayed for a while in Ephesus too, and it was here that he first met Onesiphorus.

Later on Paul was put in prison in Rome - the capital of the Roman Empire. And who do you think came to visit him? Yes, Mr. Thoughtful or Onesiphorus.

Onesiphorus heard that Paul was a prisoner, and he was concerned about him. He thought, 'Paul must be very lonely, and I am sure that he would love a visit from a friend. He would like news too of his other friends in Ephesus. Perhaps he needs

money, or food, or clothes or books. I know what I'll do, I'll find out where Paul is and I'll visit him.'

Now that was not as easy as it may sound. One-siphorus may not have been to Rome before, and it was a huge city, in which a person could easily get lost. Also about this time, there had been a fire, and many things in the city had changed.

Nevertheless, Onesiphorus went. He searched hard until he found where Paul was. He may have had great difficulty in getting permission to see him, but he managed it. It may have been danger-ous because he was letting people know that he was a Christian too, like Paul. But still he went. He was not ashamed that Paul was a prisoner, or what people may have thought about him for vis-iting someone who was a prisoner.

Paul was surprised and pleased to see him! It was not just because of the books, or the food, or the warm clothes, or the money he brought. It was because Onesiphorus' thoughtfulness showed that he really cared about Paul.

Thoughtful people think about others. Thoughtful people often do kind things people do not expect. Thoughtful people go to a lot of trouble to help others. When your mother is tired, are you thoughtful when you see a big pile of washing up in the kitchen sink?

A girl called Helen went to university. As a new student she felt very nervous and home-sick on her first day as she unpacked her things. She went to look in her mirror, and someone had written across her mirror, 'If you don't know anyone, and have nowhere to go after supper, come and have coffee in my room, number 12, at 8 pm.' It was signed 'Dorothy'. Helen's eyes blurred, and a lump filled her throat. Helen met Dorothy and discovered that she was a Christian, and a thoughtful Christian.

Christians ought to be thoughtful, because God, their Heavenly Father, is thoughtful.

The Lord Jesus, God's Son and our Saviour, showed in lots of ways how thoughtful God is. A little girl, the daughter of Jairus, died, and the Lord Jesus brought her back to life again. All the people were pleased and excited, but they all forgot something very important! But not the Lord Jesus, because He was always thoughtful. He said to them, 'Give her something to eat!' They had all forgotten that she would be hungry, as boys and girls usually are!

Even when the Lord Jesus was dying on the Cross, He was thoughtful. His mother was standing near the Cross with John, one of His disciples. He said to John, 'Look after her, please, John, as you would your own mother.'

When we become Christians, the Lord Jesus lives within us by His Spirit, and His Spirit teaches us to be thoughtful for others.

Where to read: 2 Timothy 1:16-18

Miss **Useful**

D o you know what a paper-knife is? It is a kind of knife - although not always made of metal - which we use especially for opening envelopes and letters. I have two but one does a better job than the other. One is slender and sharp, and the other is thick and blunt.

One is useful, and the other is almost useless. That is rather like our lives: they may either be useful to God and to others, or they may be of little use, and, sadly, even useless.

God wants us to be useful to Him and to other people. When we trust the Lord Jesus as our Saviour, God's purpose is always to make us useful. He gives us gifts and abilities with which we can serve others and please Him.

In the Bible God has given us lots of examples of people who were useful. We are going to think about one of them. Miss Useful's real name was Rhoda.

She lived in Jerusalem, and helped in the home of Mary, the mother of John Mark, who wrote one of the books in the Bible which tells us the good news about the Lord Jesus.

Mary was probably a widow. She needed help in the house because it was rather large, and was one of the regular meeting places for Christians in Jerusalem. Christians often met there to pray

together.

Rhoda did jobs about the house. She probably did some of the shopping, helped with the dishes, and the washing and mending of clothes.

But something dreadful happened! King Herod arrested some of the Jerusalem Christians, and he made life very difficult for them.

He had James, the brother of John, put to death with the sword. When he saw that this pleased the Jews, he decided to seize Peter too.

After arresting Peter, he put him in prison, handing him over to be guarded by four squads of soldiers.

The Christians in Jerusalem decided there was only one thing they could do, and that was to meet together to pray for Peter.

One of the places they met was Mary's home. Lots of people came to pray. As they knocked at the door, they had to be let in, and someone was needed to look after that. Who do you think had that task? Yes, Rhoda, or Miss Useful.

Backwards and forwards she ran, opening the door and letting people in to join the prayer meeting.

'Lord, please save Peter,' they must have prayed. And perhaps John Mark, who may already have started writing his gospel, prayed, 'Please keep Peter safe so that he can help me write about the Lord Jesus.'

God always answers our prayers, although not always in the way we expect. As the Christians prayed together in Mary's house, they did not know that Peter was fast asleep in the prison, bound with two chains, with sentries standing guard at the entrance.

Suddenly an angel of the Lord appeared and a

Our Bible dictionary

The gospels
The word 'gospel' means 'good news', and is a special word for the good news about the Lord Jesus. But it is also the word used to describe the four books in the Bible - by Matthew, Mark, Luke and John - which tell us the good news about the Lord Jesus' life, teaching, death and resurrection. They were written to help us understand that the Lord Jesus is God's Son, so that we might believe in Him and become God's children.

light shone in the cell. He struck Peter on the side and woke him up. 'Quick, get up!' he said. Peter's chains fell off his wrists.

Then the angel said to him, 'Put on your clothes and sandals.' And Peter did so. 'Wrap your cloak around you and follow me,' the angel told him.

Peter followed him out of the prison, but he had no idea that what the angel was doing was really happening. He thought he was seeing a vision or having a dream.

They passed through the first and second guards and came to the iron gate leading to the city. It opened for them by itself, and they went through it. When they had walked the length of one street, the angel suddenly left him.

Then Peter realized what had happened and he said, 'Now I know without a doubt that the Lord sent his angel and rescued me from Herod's clutches and from everything the Jewish people

Can you draw?

Can you draw some pictures - perhaps like a cartoon strip - of Peter's escape from prison and the Christians praying for his release. Do not forget to include Rhoda!

were hoping to do to me.'

Now there was one place he had to go to straightaway. Can you guess where it was? Yes, it was Mary's house, for Peter knew or guessed that Christians would be there praying for him.

He arrived at the house, and knocked at the outer entrance. And, of course, it was Rhoda who went to the door. She had been taught to ask, 'Who is it?' because with Christians in danger, she was only to let in those who were friends.

'Who is it?' Rhoda asked. 'It's Peter!' he replied. When Rhoda recognised Peter's voice, she was so excited and glad that without opening the door to Peter she ran back to where all the Christians were, and shouted, 'Peter is at the door!'

'You are out of your mind,' they told her. When she kept on insisting that it was so, they said, 'It must be his angel.'

But Peter kept on knocking! When they opened the door and saw him, they were astonished. Peter signalled them to be quiet and he described how the Lord had brought him out of prison.

Rhoda had been the first to know the good news! And she believed it to be Peter when others doubted. Of course, she had not been useful in opening the door to him at first, but then she had been so excited!

Even though Rhoda was only a young girl, she was useful to others, and useful in opening the door for people.

What Rhoda did saved others, who were busy, from being disturbed. What Rhoda did, though a small thing, was important.

Her faithfulness in small things must have led to greater responsibilities as she grew older. The fact that her name is mentioned in the the Bible -

remember she was only a servant-girl - probably means she became well-known among Christians in Jerusalem.

Although what Rhoda did was small, she pleased God by her faith. She had not doubted that it was Peter at the door.

When we love the Lord Jesus, we want to be useful to Him. I remember when a friend of mine, a postman, became a Christian. We wanted someone to fix small plastic holders in front of every seat in the church, in which we could put a welcome card for visitors, It was going to take hours and hours to do, and it was a really boring task. But my friend was so grateful to the Lord Jesus for dying for him, and forgiving him his sins, nothing was too much trouble for him! He became Mr. Useful. Like Rhoda, as he became useful in small things, God gave him larger things to do.

Are we useful or useless when it comes to helping and serving? If the Lord Jesus has forgiven us our sins, we will be so grateful to Him that nothing will be too much trouble if we know it is what He wants us to do. That will make us useful to God and to others.

Where to read: Acts 12:1-19

Mr **Violent**

Have you ever lost your temper, and then said and done things you have been sorry about afterwards? Most, if not all of us, have done that sometimes. Things are made worse if we are then violent, and perhaps hit out at other people.

Violence can happen very quickly if we lose our temper and do not think what we are doing. Violence is always nasty, and there is seldom an excuse for it.

People are sometimes violent in sport, and it always spoils the sport, whether it is football, rugby, cricket or any other game.

When people get drunk, they may become violent, and that is a good reason for not drinking alcohol or spirits because they take away our power to control ourselves.

Parents may sometimes make the mistake of being violent in punishing their children; and children may be violent by kicking and punching. In schools there may be bullies who like hurting other boys and girls.

A lot of violence is shown on television, and some people make video nasties which are just full of it. It is not good to look at violence on television or in films because what we watch influences the way we behave.

Christc or Messiah

'Christ' and 'Messiah' mean the same thing - 'The Anointed One'. To 'anoint' people is to pour oil on their heads, usually as a sign to show that they have been especially chosen for a task. Kings and queens are often anointed when they are crowned. The name 'Christ' or 'Messiah' is given to the Lord Jesus because God especially chose Him to be the One who would die to be the Saviour of His people.

Unfortunately it is possible to love violence, and to like being cruel. The Bible tells us not to envy violent people or choose any of their ways because it will lead us down a wrong path. God hates violence.

Several people in the Bible might be called Mr. Violent, but I have chosen Saul, or Paul as we usually call him. Saul was his Jewish name, and Paul his Roman name. We will call him Paul from now on.

He lived in the first century, and was a very religious Jew. Like all Jews, he was waiting for the Messiah, the Christ, to come. But he did not understand properly God's promises in the first half of the Bible, what we call the Old Testament, about the Messiah. He expected Him to come as a mighty King and to be someone whom everyone would immediately worship and obey.

The Lord Jesus is the Messiah, the Christ, whom God promised. When He came into the world, He lived a perfect life. He taught as no one had ever taught before. And then after three years of teaching and doing good, He died on the Cross to save us from our sins, according to God's plan. Three days after, He rose again. He had overcome sin, death, and Satan. The disciples could not have been more excited, and they went everywhere telling everyone.

But Paul did not believe what they said. He did not think that the Messiah he waited for would die on a Cross like a common criminal. Of course, Paul was wrong, but he did not understand this.

When he heard Jesus' followers telling everyone the good news that Jesus had died, and then risen again to make it possible for us to be forgiven and to become God's children, Paul was angry, and

said, 'It's not true!'

He was so filled with hatred for Christians that he tried to do them harm. He got permission from the Jewish rulers to have them arrested. He was violent to Christians in and near Jerusalem. He was cruel because he foolishly thought he was serving God by hurting them.

Christians knew their lives were in danger because of Paul. Many of them must have prayed for him.

I am glad to tell you that Paul stopped being violent after something wonderful happened in his life - something that has happened to many other people.

Mr. Violent met the one person who could change him. He met Jesus!

Paul had decided to go to Damascus to do to the Christians there what he had done in Jerusalem.

He wanted to arrest them, and bring them in chains to Jerusalem.

As he was getting close to Damascus, a bright light suddenly flashed around him. He fell to the ground and he heard a voice, 'Paul! Paul! Why are you persecuting me?' 'Who are you, Lord?' Paul asked. 'I am Jesus, whom you are persecuting! Now get up and go into the city and I will tell you

what you are to do.'

Paul knew now that he had been dreadfully wrong about Jesus. Jesus really is the Son of God, and He is alive from the dead!

Paul understood then that he had been wrong about Christians too; and he had been wrong to use violence. There and then he confessed his sins, and the Lord Jesus forgave him, and made him one of His followers.

Paul never forgot how foolish he had once been about Jesus, and about violence. He immediately told everyone he could that Jesus is the Christ, the Son of God. He spent the rest of his life serving Him and others.

Have you and I been violent? If so, we ought to be ashamed, and remember how much God hates violence. But just as the Lord Jesus forgave Paul when he realised how wrong he had been, the Lord Jesus will forgive us.

When we trust the Lord Jesus as our Saviour, He teaches us not to be violent, but self-controlled and kind. He helps us to be like Him. When people were violent against the Lord Jesus, He did not answer back with violence, but, instead, He prayed for them.

The secret of the change in our behaviour when we become Christians is that the Lord Jesus comes to live within us by His Spirit. His Spirit gives us strength to be like Jesus, and to want to do only what is kind to others.

Where to read: Acts 26:9-18
Look up too: Proverbs 3:31; Proverbs 16:29
and 1 Timothy 1:13-15.

Something to do

Mark the map!
Find where Damascus is on the map on page 46 and write in its name if you have not done so already.

Mr Walk–with–God

Mr. Walk-with-God was someone special, because he was one of the first people to love having God as his friend. He deserves a place in any book of records.

He lived in the earliest period of human history. His name was Enoch, and his great-great-great-great grandfather was Adam.

The most important thing we know about Enoch was that he walked with God. We are going to have to do some detective work to understand what the Bible means when it tells us that he walked with God but it will not be too difficult.

You often walk with other people, perhaps your Mum or Dad, or a friend. When you walk with them, you keep close to them. Enoch kept close to God, which means that he talked to God in prayer, and he gave time to God in his life.

To walk with people we keep in step with them. Enoch walked in step with God because he obeyed God. If we really want to walk with someone, we let him or her choose the way, and we follow. Enoch wanted God to choose the way he should go.

Enoch enjoyed having God as his friend, and it changed his whole life so that he became more and more like God in the way he behaved and the kind of person he was. Have you noticed how friends become like one another?

When we walk with God, His Spirit makes us more and more like Him, because we want to do what is right, and be helpful to others.

Enoch can be called Mr. Walk-with-God because he was unusual. Most other people did not walk with God. Enoch stood out because lots of other people did not even believe that God exists. Enoch not only believed God exists, but he believed that God rewards those who sincerely seek Him. And he was right!

But that did not make life easy for Enoch. He made a choice that others were not willing to

make. He walked with God when others did not. He was not afraid of being different.

Do you like being different from others? I expect not. Even with things like clothes and shoes we do not like being different from others in case people think us strange. When we go shopping for clothes we may say, 'I want that because others at school are wearing things like it.'

Enoch was willing to go against the flow of the crowd. Have you ever walked in the opposite direction to a large number of people? Perhaps you have been to a football match or a concert, and as you have begun to leave, you have remembered that you have left something behind. You have then had to go all the way back to get it, and instead of going easily in the direction of the crowd, you have gone with great difficulty in the opposite way. It is not easy! It was a bit like that for Enoch.

People probably made fun of Enoch, but he took no notice. We may think him brave; and he was. But the secret of his strength was his friendship with God.

Enoch had not always walked with God. It is here that we must do a little detective work again. How or when did he become Mr. Walk-with-God? There is just a hint in the Bible that it was the birth of his son, Methuselah, that made Enoch first think of walking with God. Perhaps it was a difficult birth, and Enoch cried to God to help his wife and baby son. Maybe he was just filled with amazement at the wonderful gift of life in a new baby.

Enoch lived many years of his life walking out of step with God, but that all changed one day. No one is born into this world walking with God. We

Something to do

Ask your parents how they felt when you were born. I would not be surprised if they felt like Enoch!

24

all begin our lives out of step with Him. That is why the Lord Jesus came into the world two thousand years ago. He came to die upon the Cross for sinners like us who have failed to walk in God's ways. When we are sorry for our sins, and trust in Him as our Saviour, He teaches us then to walk with God. He gives us His own example to follow, and His Spirit to live within our hearts to make us

Our Bible dictionary

Heaven

Heaven is where God lives. The Lord Jesus came from heaven, and returned there when His work on earth was done. It is from heaven that the Lord Jesus will come when He returns. For those who trust in the Lord Jesus it is their heavenly Father's House and their home, where one day they are going to live for ever. No-one deserves to go to heaven. The only way to heaven is through trusting in the Lord Jesus as our Saviour.

strong and courageous.

We said that Enoch was special, and deserved to be in a book of records, because he is the first person in the Bible whose special friendship with God is mentioned. But there is another reason why he was special. He is the first person who went to heaven without dying!

The Bible says that one day Enoch simply disappeared, because God took him! A girl in Sunday School put it like this: 'One day Enoch and God went out for a walk together and they got so far from Enoch's home that God said to him, "We're nearer my home than yours, why don't you come to tea?" And he did!

I do not know exactly what happened, but I know it was very wonderful for Enoch! Enoch loved God so much that nothing was better for Enoch than being with God for ever.

God has a place in heaven for everyone who walks with Him on earth.

I wonder if we are walking with God? Have we begun to walk with Him yet? The place to begin is to be sorry for not walking with Him, and to ask the Lord Jesus to be our Saviour. Then He gives us strength to walk with God.

Where to read: Genesis 5:18-24; Hebrews 11:1-6

Mr <u>X</u>–Ray

X is probably the most difficult letter in the alphabet for which to find a Bible character! But I have thought of someone whom we may call Mr. X-Ray.

An X-Ray is the name given to an important discovery in 1896 by a Professor called Routgen. He used the letter 'X' to indicate that neither he nor anyone else could understand how these invisible rays worked, but they did understand what X-Rays could do. 'X' stood for something they were sure of, but which they could not explain. So they called the rays they discovered X-Rays.

Security officers at airports X-Ray people's

belongings. They use X-Ray machines to search for illegal goods such as bombs or drugs. Each piece of luggage is X-Rayed before being loaded on board a plane.

Every day of the week in hospitals around the world people have X-Rays. They provide a special photograph of our bodies so that doctors can see if there is anything wrong.

Have you ever had an X-Ray? If we break an arm or a leg, doctors will want us to have an X-Ray before they try to put things straight.

An X-Ray is a way of seeing things which would otherwise be hidden or secret. That is why I am

Apostles

An apostle is someone sent out as a messenger. Although it can mean any sort of messenger, it describes the men the Lord Jesus first chose to be His special followers so that they might be eye-witnesses of His life and work, and especially of His resurrection.

Do you remember?

Jerusalem
See page 19.

calling the apostle Peter Mr. X-Ray.

Let me tell what happened. In the early days of the Church in Jerusalem, many people became Christians, and some were poor and others were better off and even rich. Those who believed in the Lord Jesus shared everything with each other, and cared for one another.

No one was allowed to be poor because many who owned land or houses sold them, or part of them, and brought the money to the apostles for them to give to people in need. It was a kind and generous thing to do.

But here we come to the sad part of the story. A husband and wife did a silly thing. A man called Ananias decided to sell a property that he had, and to give some of the money he got for it to the poor. But when he brought the money to the apostles, he pretended that it was all the money he had received. Sapphira, his wife, agreed with what he did.

It was a foolish idea. Ananias and Sapphira did not need to give all of money from their property to God for His people. But they wanted others to think them more generous than they were. They were deceitful. They were really telling a lie.

But they had forgotten something important. God sees and knows everything! He can see what no one else can see. He can 'X-Ray' our minds and hearts, even better than doctors can X-Ray our bodies.

Ananias and Sapphira had also forgotten something else. God gives His Holy Spirit to those who trust the Lord Jesus as their Saviour, and obey Him. God's Spirit lived in Peter and the other apostles, to whom Ananias brought his gift of money for God.

30

As soon as Ananias came with the money, Peter knew something was wrong. He was filled with the Holy Spirit and he saw through Ananias' deceit. God gave Peter X-Ray eyes so that he saw what ordinary eyes could not see.

Peter said, 'Ananias, how is it that Satan has so filled your heart that you have lied to the Holy Spirit and have kept for yourself some of the money you received for the land? Didn't it belong to you before it was sold? And after it was sold, wasn't the money yours to do with what you wanted? What made you think of doing such a thing? You have not lied to men, but to God.'

When Ananias heard this, he fell down and died. And exactly the same thing happened to Sapphira, his wife.

It was because Peter was filled with God's Spirit that he saw through Ananias and Sapphira's lie, and knew what Satan had put into their hearts to do. Peter was Mr. X-Ray because he was filled with the Holy Spirit.

It is always good to remember that God sees what no one else can see. He knows all our thoughts. He knows what we are going to say even before we say it!

God also helps His servants to see what cannot be seen by the human eye when it is important for them to do so. We call this insight. It is a gift God gives by His Spirit.

We can never deceive God. We often cannot deceive those in whom God's Spirit lives.

One of the most wonderful things about being a Christian is that God's Holy Spirit comes to live within us. He helps us to see and understand things we would not otherwise be able to see and understand. Most of all He helps us to understand the Bible, and to know that the Lord Jesus is always near to help us.

If only Ananias and Sapphira had really trusted the Lord Jesus as their Saviour, and allowed His Spirit to fill their lives! Then - like Peter - they would known that possessing the Lord Jesus is much more valuable and precious than any piece of land or property! The Holy Spirit is a wonderful gift to every Christian from our heavenly Father and our Saviour, the Lord Jesus.

Where to read: Acts 4:32-5:10

Our Bible Dictionary

The Holy Spirit

There is only one true God, and He is one in three distinct Persons, Father, Son and Holy Spirit.

The Holy Spirit is God, and He is the Third Person of the Trinity. The Trinity - three in unity - is the name we give to this special oneness that God has in Three Persons.

It is not easy for us to understand, but we must remember that we are talking about God who is very great, and our minds are much too small to understand everything about Him.

The Holy Spirit has given us the Bible because He prompted the writers to write, and made sure that they wrote only what is true.

33

Mr **Yawner**

Something to do

Mark the map!
Find where Troas and Troy are on the map on page 47 and write in their names.

What does it mean to yawn? When we yawn we open our mouth wide to draw in air. It shows we are either tired or bored! See if you can do a yawn ! That now makes us all like Mr. Yawner whom we are going to think about!

Mr. Yawner was a young man, and his real name was Eutychus. In his own Greek language, his name meant 'Lucky'.

He lived in a city called Troas, near the old city of Troy. It was a Roman colony, and was the port for travellers from Asia to Europe.

Paul visited Troas for a week. His last day there was a Sunday.

Why is Sunday so important to Christians? Yes, because it is in a special way God's Day. Each Sunday we remember how God created everything, and then rested on the seventh day.

It is also the day on which our Lord Jesus rose again from the dead, and every Sunday we remember His rising again and that He lives for ever!

In Troas all the Christians met together on a Sunday to worship God. But they were not able to do this as easily as we do.

Many of them were slaves. That meant that they had to work hard all day, and every day, and they

Our Bible dictionary

A Christian

People who believe in the Lord Jesus were first called Christians as a nick-name. Christians are those who belong to the Lord Jesus because they know that He died for their sins and rose again to be their Saviour and Lord. It is another name for those who follow the Lord Jesus.

could only meet to worship God with other Christians when their daily work was done.

They did not have church buildings like most of us, but they met in an upstairs room, on the third floor. Perhaps you live in a block of flats with several floors or your school has more than one storey.

The Christians met together first to remember the Lord Jesus in what we call the Lord's Supper or the Communion Service. And then they listened to God's Word being taught and preached.

On this occasion when Paul was there, he preached. As he was leaving the next day, there was a lot he wanted to talk to them about.

And so he preached a long time! For lights, they had oil lamps. They not only gave light, but they gave off heat.

The room grew hotter and hotter. The flickering lamps and warm atmosphere caused by all the people being squashed into one room made it difficult to keep awake, and especially for those who had been working hard all day.

Eutychus was probably already tired when he arrived, but he wanted to hear God's Word. He went and sat in the window. As the room became warmer and warmer, Eutychus' eyes began to close, and his head began to fall - and then he jerked himself up to try to keep awake. But soon he fell asleep again.

And then something dreadful happened! He fell out of the window down into the street below. When everyone ran down to see if they could help him, they found that he was dead.

Paul went down too. He took the young man up into his arms. Then a miracle took place! Paul said, 'Don't be alarmed. He is alive!'

How pleased and delighted all the Christians were! Paul then carried on preaching!

What do we learn from Eutychus, Mr. Yawner? Never sit in a window, especially if it is above the first floor!

But there are other important lessons. It is a great gift and privilege to be able to have Sundays free from school and work so that we can join with others to worship God and hear His Word.

Our Bible dictionary

The Lord's Supper

At the Lord's Supper Christians eat bread and drink wine, as the first disciples did on the night the Lord Jesus was betrayed. The bread and the wine are symbols or pictures of the Lord Jesus' body and blood. Another name for the Lord's Supper is the Communion Service - 'communion' means fellowship or sharing. At the Lord's Supper Christians remember with gratitude how they share in the wonderful benefits that come to them through the Lord Jesus' death for them - especially the forgiveness of sins. They also look forward to the time when the Lord Jesus comes again to take all His people to be with Him for ever.

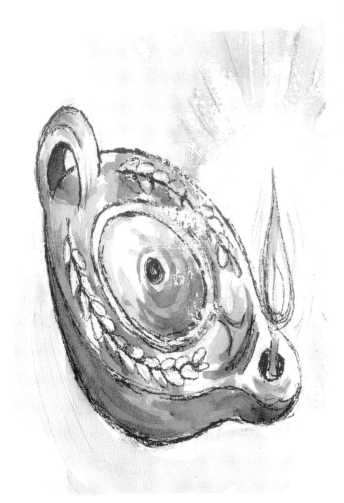

Draw Eutychus sitting on the widow ledge, yawning.

No matter how busy we are, we should always meet with God's people on His Day.

Eutychus probably could not help yawning. But we often can help it, can't we? The best preparation for Sunday is an early night to bed on a Saturday. Sometimes we cannot help being Master or Miss Yawner because we have had to be up late for some good reason. But let us try to make sure that it is not our fault!

Where to read: Acts 20:6-12

38

Mr Zoo keeper

There is really no doubt about whom we may call Mr. Zoo-keeper in the Bible. It is Noah who built an ark for the animals and his family.

The word 'zoo' comes from the first three letters of the word 'zoological'.

Zoologists is the name given to scientists who study animals, and care about them.

Noah cared very much about the animals he took into his large wooden boat. But behind his care of the animals, there was a very sad story. The wickedness of men and women in the world had become great, and was getting worse and worse.

God decided to punish the world with a flood. But there was one man who really did trust in God and who wanted to please Him, and that was Noah.

God decided to save Noah and his family, together with some of every kind of bird and animal so that there might be a new beginning for the world.

God told Noah how to build a great boat, called an ark. It was 450 feet long, 75 feet wide and 45 feet high.

God told Noah to take two of all living creatures, male and female, to keep them alive with him, whether they were birds that flew or animals

Can you draw?

Draw an ark with Noah, his family, and the animals going into it.

40

that moved along the ground. Some kinds of animal God chose for Noah and his family and the animals to eat, and so God told him to take more of each of these.

As well as that, he had to collect and store away every kind of food for each of them. What a job!

The flood came just as God promised. Noah, and his family, and all the animals in the ark, were kept safe.

God judged the world in such a serious way because of the bad things that men and women did. Their sin brought harm to the animals and birds as well as to boys and girls, and men and women.

That is true today, isn't it? When we pollute the atmosphere, spoil the countryside, we bring harm to God's creatures. That is why some birds and animals are now extinct.

God chose Noah to be Mr. Zoo-Keeper to show us that He cares about animals. He told Noah to take the right food for each of them.

We too ought to care for all God's creatures.

We should think about them, just as God thought about not only Noah in the ark, but the birds and animals too.

It is thoughtful to feed the birds in winter, and to keep our animals indoors when events like firework displays are taking place.

Noah was Mr. Zoo-Keeper because God knew that we need animals. We need some for the help they give us, and others for food.

Animals are often company for people. Our pets become good friends. Animals also provide us with food to eat.

Noah was Mr. Zoo-Keeper too because God used certain animals as pictures of the Lord Jesus.

Some of the extra animals Noah took into the ark he offered as a sacrifice when he came out of it.

The death of those animals could never take away sins, but it was God's way of preparing the

Did you know?

The rainbow
Do you know what we are meant to remember every time we see a rainbow? Look up what God said to Noah and his sons in Genesis 9:8-17

Something to do

Make a short list of some pets who can be good company

1. hapster = rgash
2. Sunshine Author queene = rubi
3. Fish

43

world for the coming of the Lord Jesus, the Lamb of God, who can take away our sins.

So there are helpful lessons we learn from Noah, Mr. Zoo-Keeper.

Whenever we see wild animals, who make us afraid, we should remember that it was human sin in the beginning that made them like that. Adam and Eve's sin spoiled the whole of God's creation.

We should care about animals, and look after them. God does, and He wants us to share His

care.

And, most of all, we should thank God for the Lord Jesus, the Lamb of God, for whose coming even Noah prepared the way as he took animals like sheep and lambs into the ark.

Where to read: Genesis 6:5-22

MEDITERRANEAN
SEA
(The Great Sea)

DᴜMᴀSᴄᴜS

GALILEE

Sea
of
Galilee

ISRAEL
(Palestine)

●CAESAREA

JEZREEL

SAMARIA

●TEL AVIV

JOPPA
(JAFFA)

LYDDA

JERICHO

JERUSALEM

Dead
Sea

BETHANY

MAMRE

MAON

SODOM

GAZA
DESERT

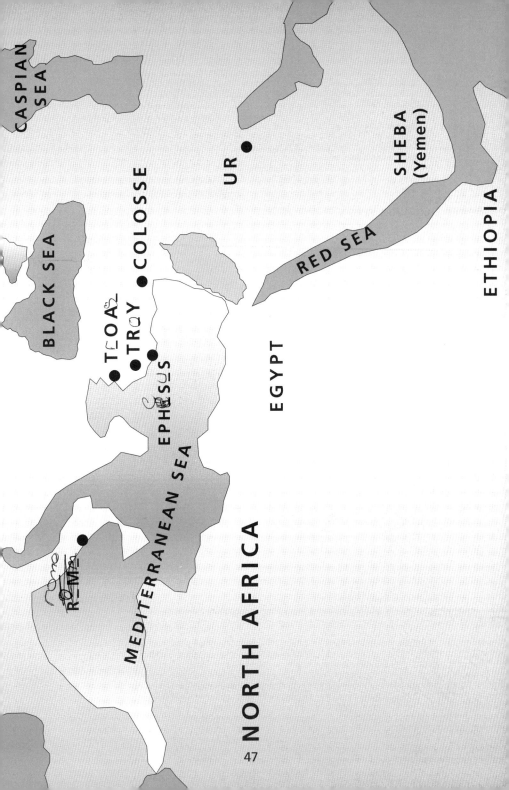

CASPIAN SEA

BLACK SEA

UR

SHEBA
(Yemen)

RED SEA

ETHIOPIA

COLOSSE

TROAS

TROY

EPHESUS

EGYPT

MEDITERRANEAN SEA

Rome
ROME

NORTH AFRICA

47